Ride Right

Bicycle Safety

How to Be Safe!

by Jill Urban Donahue   illustrated by Bob Masheris

PICTURE WINDOW BOOKS
Minneapolis, Minnesota

Special thanks to our advisers for their expertise:
Preston Tyree, Director of Education
League of American Bicyclists

Terry Flaherty, Ph.D., Professor of English
Minnesota State University, Mankato

Editor: Jill Kalz
Designer: Abbey Fitzgerald
Page Production: Melissa Kes
Art Director: Nathan Gassman
Associate Managing Editor: Christianne Jones
The illustrations in this book were created digitally.

Picture Window Books
151 Good Counsel Drive
P.O. Box 669
Mankato, MN 56002-0669
877-845-8392
www.picturewindowbooks.com

Printed in the United States of America.

All books published by Picture Window Books
are manufactured with paper containing at least
10 percent post-consumer waste.

Library of Congress Cataloging-in-Publication Data
Donahue, Jill L. (Jill Lynn), 1967-
Ride right : bicycle safety / by Jill Urban Donahue ;
illustrated by Bob Masheris.
p. cm. – (How to be safe!)
Includes index.
ISBN-13: 978-1-4048-4817-7 (library binding)
1. Cycling—Safety measures—Juvenile literature.
2. Bicycles—Safety measures—Juvenile literature.
I. Masheris, Robert, ill. II. Title.
GV1055.D67 2009
796.6028'9–dc22   2008006421

Bicycle riding is fun! It's a great way to get around. It's good exercise, too. But you need to be careful so you don't get hurt. If you follow bike safety rules, you'll have a great time.

Ajay gets a new bike from his parents for his birthday. He can't wait to ride it. First, his dad tells him the rules of the road.

Ajay listens carefully. He wants to be safe.

Safety Tip

Riders who are 10 years old or younger should ride only on the sidewalk.

Ajay's sister gives him another birthday present. It's a new helmet! Ajay's sister says he should never ride a bike without a helmet. She helps Ajay put on the helmet and makes sure it fits well.

Safety Tip

Helmet straps should be snug under your chin. When you open your mouth wide, your helmet should move.

Next, Ajay's mom adjusts the bike for Ajay. She checks the seat height and the brakes. She also checks the reflectors on the front and back of Ajay's bike.

Safety Tip

Seats should be adjusted so that both of your feet can easily reach the ground while you're sitting on the seat. The handlebars should be easy to reach, too.

9

Ajay's brother has one last gift. He gives Ajay a sporty shirt to wear while riding his bike. It has reflector stripes on the sleeves. The stripes reflect light and make Ajay easier to see.

Safety Tip

Light-colored clothing is the safest for you to wear while riding your bike. It helps other people see you clearly.

Before Ajay takes a ride, his dad shows him the hand signals he should use.

Ajay puts his left arm straight out before turning left.

He bends his left arm up before turning right.

Safety Tip

In some states, you can put your right arm straight out to show you are turning right.

13

Near the corner, Ajay bends his left arm at the elbow. His hand points down. This hand signal shows that Ajay is stopping.

Safety Tip
Always ride in a single-file line.

Ajay checks for traffic before he crosses the street.
He looks left, right, and left again.

Ice C

Safety Tip

Always remember to walk your bike across the street.

Ajay and his dad stop for an ice-cream cone.
They lock up their bikes outside the shop.

Ice Cream

When the sun starts to set, Ajay and his dad ride home. Dad says it is not safe for kids to ride at night.

Safety Tip

Biking at night is always dangerous and should be avoided. Older riders who do bike at night should have a headlight and taillight on their bikes.

A ball bounces out of a driveway, right in front of Ajay. He sees it and stops his bike in time.

Ajay avoids crashes. He pays attention to things going on around him.

Ajay is a safe and alert bicycle rider!

To Learn More

More Books to Read

Barraclough, Sue. *Bicycle Safety*. Chicago: Heinemann Library, 2008.

Leaney, Cindy. *Look Out! A Story About Safety on Bicycles*. Vero Beach, Fla.: Rourke Pub., 2004.

Mattern, Joanne. *Staying Safe on My Bike*. Milwaukee: Weekly Reader Early Learning Library, 2007.

Pancella, Peggy. *Bicycle Safety*. Chicago: Heinemann Library, 2005.

On the Web

FactHound offers a safe, fun way to find Web sites related to topics in this book. All of the sites on FactHound have been researched by our staff.

1. Visit www.facthound.com
2. Type in this special code: 1404848177
3. Click on the FETCH IT button.

Your trusty FactHound will fetch the best sites for you!

Index

Look for all of the books in the How to Be Safe! series:

Contain the Flame: Outdoor Fire Safety

Play It Safe: Playground Safety

Ride Right: Bicycle Safety

Say No and Go: Stranger Safety